FULLY ALIVE!

YOUR PERSONAL JOURNEY INTO DISCOVERING HIDDEN MYSTERIES

JOHN PAUL JACKSON

FULLY ALIVE!
Your Personal Journey Into Discovering Hidden Mysteries
By John Paul Jackson

Published by Streams Publishing House
www.streamsministries.com
1-888-441-8080

This book incorporates content from John Paul Jackson's television series "Dreams and Mysteries" and other sources.

ISBN: 978-0-9858638-6-9
Printed in the United States of America

FOR MORE INFORMATION:
USA: www.streamsministries.com
Canada: www.streamscanada.com
1-888-441-8080

DEDICATION

To dreamers who want to explore and for explorers who seek answers to mysteries.

CONTENTS

CHAPTER 1

THE MYSTERY OF JUSTICE

What is justice? What does it look like? That question could depend on which side of the courtroom you're standing on. On the part of the plaintiff, it might look a lot like revenge. For the defendant, it probably looks more like mercy.

In the end, somebody "wins" and somebody "loses." One side feels justice was served. The other may feel that justice was not served.

Do you need justice? What is your definition of justice? Chances are that your definition might change based on how it has played out in your life. Bad things do happen to good people, and seemingly good things happen to bad people. Where is the justice in that?

The justice of man isn't always rendered even when a decision is made. The justice of man is limited to the knowledge of man. The problem is that the knowledge of man keeps changing with additional knowledge.

The justice of God, however, is based on the knowledge of God, which never changes. God is all-knowing, omniscient. Being "all-knowing" means God has never lost knowledge or gained knowledge. His omniscience makes God's justice infinitely superior to man's justice.

God created you to have a deep desire to see justice take place. You desire it for yourself as well as for others. According to Scripture, the very throne of God rests on two pillars—righteousness and justice.

Clouds and darkness surround Him; Righteousness and justice are the foundation of His throne.

PSALM 97:2

Here is the good news: God wants you to receive justice for the injustices that have happened to you. How would you go about that? You have to know God's judicial process. You won't need a lawyer.

Remember, God's law library only has one volume, and you probably already own it.

Have you ever been through periods or seasons of your life when you felt that God must have been angry with you, times when you felt everything was much more difficult than it had to be, times when you felt the enemy must have been after you?

Those are the times God uses to mold your character. It is not wrong to ask when you are in the middle of those times, "Where is the justice?" There has to be a balance, right? We can feel it deep inside when the scales of justice have been tipped in one direction.

So the question we need to ask in those trying times is, "Why is God allowing this?" Why would a good God allow me to be attacked by the enemy?

This is the mystery of God's justice. When the scales of justice have tipped out of your favor, how do you get them get tipped back into balance?

A scale can be balanced in two ways. Either we can remove some weight from one side, or we can add weight to the other side. What if God's justice worked the same way? What if God was waiting to tip the scales back into your favor? Injustice has happened, and He wants to do something to bring it back into balance.

The process we see in scripture does this very thing. There is divine justice, and God has given us keys to receiving His justice. When you follow these keys, you activate a process that can help you get back what the enemy has stolen from you and your family.

The real mystery of God's justice might be how something as complex as a system of justice could also be so perfect in its simplicity. To understand it, we have to understand that there is a process. God has hidden keys in His Word to receive His justice—hidden, like many of His mysteries, in plain sight.

Before Jesus died and was resurrected, justice wasn't anything that a normal person would have wanted any part of. We would have wanted mercy, sure. Justice just wasn't a subject we would want to bring up. God gave laws and statutes to Moses so he could render judgment. Back then, before Christ paid for our sins on the cross, justice was harsh. If you came to God seeking justice, the ground could open up, and someone would not be home for dinner that night.

BEFORE THE CROSS, JUSTICE WAS HARSH. JESUS TOOK THE JUDGMENT UPON HIMSELF.

The power of the cross is that Jesus took that judgment upon Himself. When we believe in our hearts that Jesus did this, we gain salvation. Salvation comes with "diplomatic immunity" against the eternal judgment of our sins. This is a pretty big reason to believe on the Lord Jesus Christ and be saved.

God's justice then gets even bigger. When there is justice that is owed to us, we can literally place a claim for it. Justice waits for us like an escrow account in Heaven. What if I told you the Righteous Judge is waiting to hear your claim against your adversary? What if God provided justice even for something that didn't happen to you? What if it was something that happened to your ancestors?

Our problem is that if we don't make the claim, He can't render a decision.

As you may know, injustice can come in a variety of ways, and it leaves a lasting mark. We tend to forget about justice when we get away with something we shouldn't have done, but we always remember justice when we didn't get something we thought we deserved. We are acutely aware of justice when we are accused of something we didn't do. When we look back at the Old Testament, we see something very interesting about justice. Prophets would cry out to God for it. Why is that significant? Because God wanted to give justice, but others were not asking for it, or did not know how.

Prophets were to cry out for justice, and priests were to ensure God's justice was applied. Kings and apostles were tasked with carrying out justice. The importance of God's law of justice was always to be recognized and understood. Those who broke the law knew what the consequences were for their actions. From the rich to the poor, from the politician to the servant, everyone was expected to know the truth and understand the consequences of justice.

Today, could we be at a place where God is reminding us to cry out for justice? I believe so, because we are not crying out for justice enough. Our problem today is that many times we don't believe we deserve justice.

We can fall into a trap of thinking that we haven't done enough for God to act on our behalf. This is a trap because it is impossible for anyone to ever do enough. No one ever has.

The enemy will use this and other lies to do his best to convince us that we're not worthy of God giving us justice. The enemy wants to keep us as a victim and viewing our world with a victim mentality. The enemy will do his best to convince

"YET THEY SEEK ME DAILY, AND DELIGHT TO KNOW MY WAYS... THEY ASK OF ME THE ORDINANCES OF JUSTICE; THEY TAKE DELIGHT IN APPROACHING GOD."
ISAIAH 58:2

"JUSTICE FOR MAN COMES FROM THE LORD."
PROVERBS 29:26

"SEEK JUSTICE, REBUKE THE OPPRESSOR; DEFEND THE FATHERLESS, PLEAD FOR THE WIDOW."
ISAIAH 1:17

us that we don't deserve God's justice. However, God's Word says differently. His Word says we can have justice, and it just requires us to ask for it.

What makes up the foundation of God's throne? Justice and righteousness

Let's look at a very real example. In the United States, the families of the victims of the terrorist attack on the World Trade Center known as 9/11 have a settlement fund. It is the desire of the U.S. government to compensate those victims for the unexpected and unjust loss they experienced due to that enemy attack.

Not a single one of those family members ever received a check automatically in the mail. Instead, they had to go through steps that were set up to prove they were eligible. Then they had to follow a process and fill out the necessary paperwork. They had to appear before a judicial panel. Then they had to wait to receive their allotted settlement. For those who did not receive their settlement in what they thought was a timely manner, they had to keep calling and checking on the status of their claim.

What would happen to those deserving individuals if they never filled out the paperwork? What if they followed the process incorrectly? What if they never followed up with a telephone call to ensure they were on the right track? They may have never received a settlement.

What about you? Do you deserve justice? Do you need to get justice for something that has happened to you? Has someone stolen from you? Have you been passed over for a promotion you deserved? Have you been slandered, or lied about, or has that happened to a member of your family? Have you lost contracts due to bribery? Has the enemy overplayed his hand by attacking you when he had no legal reason for the attack? This is all part of the justice that God wants to bring to you and your family.

God sees the impact injustice has in each individual life. Some of the poor decisions people make are due to injustices they received in their past.

Do you have hopes that some sort of universal justice, something like karma, will balance the scales? For many people, it seems easier to imagine that the universe has its own version of justice. This causes people to say things like, "What goes around comes around."

Believing in the "karma" of the universe will not bring justice to you. Karma is just a Hindu principle that is directly tied to a belief in reincarnation. This is a classic example of pseudo-spirituality. False spirituality takes a true spiritual principle and then counterfeits it to promote a philosophy that doesn't need God.

The truth is, the universe doesn't automatically give justice, and neither does Mother Nature. Just looking at the condition of the world around us, we can see for ourselves that there is no cosmic judge dispensing justice equally to all.

God wants to balance the scales of justice for you. God is waiting to enforce the laws of the Kingdom against the perpetrator who has wronged you. That perpetrator is Satan, but you can't expect this just to happen. You have to ask in order to receive God's justice. God loves justice. He is passionate about it. His Word is full of it. He promises to make sure you receive it if you meet some simple conditions. God has steps you and I must follow to receive His justice, whether the injustice we've experienced has been due to people or from powers of darkness.

The first key to receiving God's justice is forgiveness. Before we ask God for justice, we need to make sure that we are innocent before Him. Jesus did pay the price for our sin on the cross, but this isn't a salvation issue. We're asking God to be justified to act on our behalf. This means we are asking God to forgive and cleanse us of every sin.

That's not the end of it. We also have to forgive those who have wronged us. This might be the hardest thing to do. We may find it easy to ask God to forgive us, but what about forgiving someone else? That often proves to be much more difficult. It is often the hardest thing we will ever do. We have to forgive the very person or persons who wronged us, even though they are the very reason we're even asking God for justice!

Peter came to Him and said, "Lord, how often shall my brother sin against me, and I forgive him? Up to seven times?" Jesus said to him, "I do not say to you, up to seven times, but up to seventy times seven."

MATTHEW 18:21-22

Why is forgiving others such a big deal to God? It's a matter of the heart. We can't expect God to forgive others when we don't forgive. Peter asked Jesus how many times he needed to forgive. Jesus responded, "Seventy times seven." Does that really mean that we should forgive everyone who has trespassed against us 490 times? Probably not.

We can look at the numbers, as some do, with seven being God's "perfect" number, and conclude that we must keep forgiving until we're free from the burden of the feelings. Regardless of how we want to interpret this particular scripture, Jesus' statement illustrates how huge an issue forgiving others is to God and how it affects our relationship with God.

Forgiveness is not denying that the injustice occurred. Forgiveness is not letting the other person off the hook as if they were not responsible. Forgiveness is acknowledging what occurred and letting it go. Forgiveness means not trying to hold the person captive for what they did. Unforgiveness holds us captive.

Unforgiveness is more than an emotion. It's like a poison we drink every day. We may wish the person who hurt us would be harmed, but we're the ones drinking the poison! Withholding forgiveness can affect our spirits, minds, emotions, relationships with others, and even our health. Unforgiveness and bitterness can lead to depression, anxiety, high blood pressure and a host of associated illnesses such as ulcers and heart disease.

Why would we forgive someone we're asking God to judge? We're actually not asking God to judge that person. We're asking God for justice. It's not the same thing. Justice is not revenge.

JUSTICE IS NOT REVENGE.

How God handles the person who has treated us unjustly is completely up to Him. What we're asking for is to have what was stolen from us returned in whatever way God sees fit. We're asking Him to compensate us for the pain, heal our hearts, give us back the time, and restore the relationships we lost due to the injustice. Until we forgive, we have made ourselves the judge. It's only when we forgive that we allow God to be the judge. After we've completely forgiven all those who have hurt us, we can ask God for His justice.

That's when we tell Him, "It's not right what happened! Justice has not been served. Father, please act on my behalf and give me justice."

The most important key to justice is the key of forgiveness.

SOMETIMES, GOD REVEALS THE REASON WE'RE NOT GETTING JUSTICE THROUGH A DREAM....

The dreamer has a recurring dream. In it, a friend that she hasn't talked to in years shows up at the back door of her house and tries to get in. The dreamer doesn't want to let her in because she doesn't feel like talking to her, but the old friend keeps trying to open the door and occasionally asks the dreamer through the door to unlock it. The dreamer thinks about calling the police, but doesn't think they will do anything because the dreamer knows the woman and they used to be friends. At this point, the dreamer starts to get very angry and begins yelling for the woman to go away. She runs into a closet and starts screaming. The dreamer recalls several dreams where she has run into a closet to scream. When she wakes up, she is still angry.

Not every dream will be telling us something wonderful about ourselves, or that something great is coming to us in the future. This dream is one that tells us the condition we're in. It is literally called a "self-condition dream." It is one of the twenty common categories of dreams.

It is very normal for people to have a dream like this. In fact, this kind of dream shows the incredible love God has for us because He reveals things about us that we don't even know about ourselves. This is why it is called a "self-condition dream."

God reveals the state of our hearts so we can pray for God to help us change the issue that is holding us back.

A SELF-CONDITION DREAM REVEALS THE STATE OF YOUR HEART.

Houses in dreams represent your life. A front door represents things in the future, while a back door or back porch represents things from the past.

In this dream, something is trying to come back into the dreamer's life—something from the past, an old friend, something the dreamer is familiar with.

Because dreams are like parables, they are almost always metaphorical. This old friend might not literally be trying to come back into the dreamer's life as a friend. Instead, the "old friend" could signify an old issue or memory from the dreamer's past that she doesn't want to deal with. In fact, the dreamer may be familiar with it, but she may have put off dealing with the issue on more than one occasion. That issue may have something to do with a friend who hurt her, or some hurts in her past.

The dreamer mentioned that she thought about calling the police, but since she knew the person, she didn't think the police would do anything. Police officers in dreams frequently represent authority. The dreamer wants to call the authority, but she's not sure the authority will act.

DREAMS ARE LIKE PARABLES. THEY ARE ALMOST ALWAYS METAPHORICAL.

The issue she's facing is from her past and is something close to her. It might be unforgiveness. It might be a wound that was inflicted or a misunderstanding that never got straightened out or made right. If it is, a higher authority cannot remove that for the dreamer. It has to start with her. God cannot put forgiveness in our hearts, but He can cause us to want to forgive.

POLICE OFFICERS REPRESENT AUTHORITY, OFTEN GOD.

Finally, the dreamer runs into the closet to scream. These issues from her past cause anger to mount up in her

GOD CANNOT PUT FORGIVENESS IN OUR HEARTS, BUT HE CAN CAUSE US TO WANT TO FORGIVE.

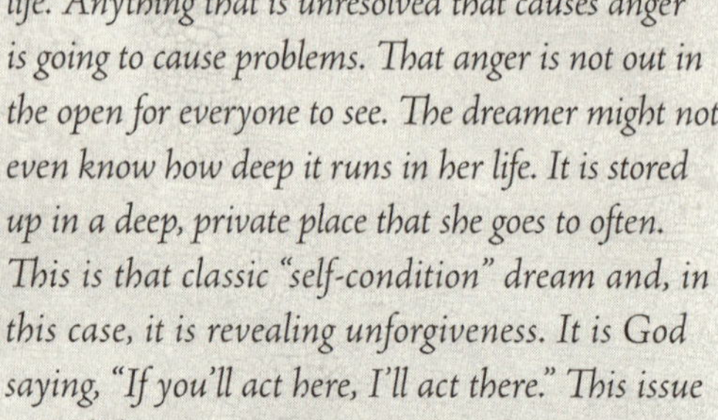

life. Anything that is unresolved that causes anger is going to cause problems. That anger is not out in the open for everyone to see. The dreamer might not even know how deep it runs in her life. It is stored up in a deep, private place that she goes to often. This is that classic "self-condition" dream and, in this case, it is revealing unforgiveness. It is God saying, "If you'll act here, I'll act there." This issue is so important to God that He went through the effort to design a dream so the dreamer could forgive this person and release herself from the awful burden of anger and bitterness. The dream was sent to let her out of the deep, dark place where she was spiritually bound. ■

After we've asked for forgiveness from God and forgiven others, we're ready for the next key to receiving God's justice. That is, we have to catch the thief.

The Bible says we have to catch the thief. When we catch him, the idea is then to bring him before the magistrate and tell the court what the thief has done. When we do, depending on the offense, we can receive two to seven times what the thief stole from us.

The key is we have to catch the thief. If we don't catch him, we don't receive justice, so the question becomes how do we catch the thief?

First, we have to recognize that what happened to us was not God. It was the evil one. The evil one stole from us. The evil one intruded in our lives. We bring this issue before the righteous judge. We present what was stolen from us, and who stole it from us, and we ask God for justice.

Have you lost money, time, peace, friendships, your health? All of these losses can be repaid up to seven times.

We have to recognize that what happened was not from God. It had to be evil. That's how we catch the thief. We recognize the intrusion of evil in our lives.

There is one condition to receiving God's justice. The condition is that the enemy has to have intruded upon us. What does that mean? Intrusion means it's not our fault. We didn't open the door to the evil one to steal from us. He broke in.

The enemy attacks us in two ways, by intrusion or invitation. Invitation means we've left a door open and the enemy has used that door to harass and steal from us. What does an open door look like?

Pride, greed, lust, guilt or fear can be doors the enemy uses to steal from us and our family. If we're experiencing injustice in our lives, we need to search our hearts and look for any doors that we have left open.

Invitation is the same as giving your keys to the thief, and then trying to claim he stole your car. If we have left no doors open, this is an intrusion, and this deserves justice.

"IF A MAN DELIVERS TO HIS NEIGHBOR MONEY OR ARTICLES TO KEEP, AND IT IS STOLEN OUT OF THE MAN'S HOUSE, IF THE THIEF IS FOUND, HE SHALL PAY DOUBLE."

EXODUS 22:7

"PEOPLE DO NOT DESPISE A THIEF IF HE STEALS TO SATISFY HIMSELF WHEN HE IS STARVING. YET WHEN HE IS FOUND, HE MUST RESTORE SEVENFOLD."

PROVERBS 6:30-31

INTRUSION IS AN ILLEGAL ACT OF ENTERING, SEIZING, OR TAKING POSSESSION OF ANOTHER'S PROPERTY.]

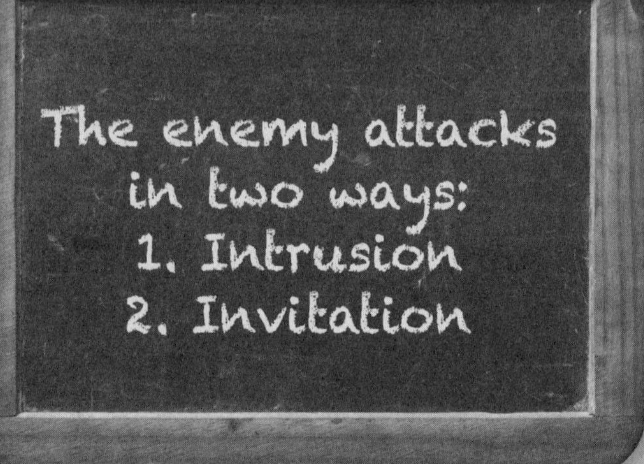

The last key to receiving God's justice is to keep asking for it. Jesus told a parable of the persistent widow who wanted justice against her adversary. She wanted it so badly that she pounded on the door of the unrighteous judge until she received justice.

The question becomes how badly do you want justice? Ask for it night and day. Continue to bring it before God. Just as Jesus taught in the parable, if an unrighteous judge will respond to persistence, how much more will the Righteous Judge of all the universe respond to you when you ask?

Receiving God's justice is up to us. It requires us to do something that we may not feel we have the strength to do.

Keys to God's Justice
1. Make sure you are innocent before God
2. Catch the thief
3. Keep asking for it

It requires us to recognize that justice is available to us. It also requires that we let go of any pain we've been holding onto and all unforgiveness. Unforgiveness is the poison we drink every day hoping it makes someone else sick. It won't. Seeking justice is not seeking revenge. Seeking justice is what returns the scales to balance.

Yes, you've been lied to. You've been lied about. You've been used. You've felt thrown away. You've had relationships dissolve, or even ripped away before their time. God's justice is not based on revenge for those acts. God's justice is based on His great love for you.

None of this has taken God by surprise. He longs to give you justice. He's waiting for you to cry out for that justice. He wants to return to you what was stolen. His capacity to give you justice far exceeds your ability to get justice for yourself. Justice comes in many packages. It doesn't always look like what we expect.

What if the answer to your cry for justice wasn't what you expected? What if it was that your neighbor suddenly, unexpectedly, asks you to tell him about God? What if that happened at the post office, or at a gas station? What if the settlement that was rendered on your behalf involved the healing of someone you've never met? Would this be justice to you?

We don't know the way the weights will be balanced and justice will happen. The ways of God are mysterious. Now you get to be part of that mystery, as you ask for justice.

Reflections and Meditations

Have you had an injustice happen to you that is still affecting you today?

Does true justice exist today? How do you respond when injustices happen to you?

Do you find it hard to forgive others? Is there someone in your life that you believe you could never forgive?

How would forgiving that person affect your ability to receive justice?

What could you do today to start the process in your life of giving forgiveness and receiving justice?

CHAPTER 2

THE MYSTERY OF DREAMS

Encoded within the design of mankind is the desire to know more. We want to know more about ourselves, others, our surroundings, the universe, God. It comes as no surprise that the human mind, prone to curiosity, delights in solving mysteries. Some mysteries are devised by men—suspense novels, card tricks, vanishing acts. Such mysteries make us wonder, "How did they do that?" We are hard-wired to ask, "What's going to happen next?"

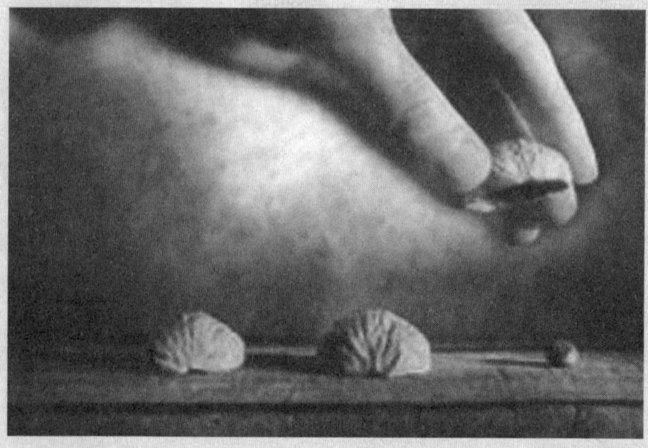

Some mysteries are hidden within creation and life itself. These are mysteries that science and man's logic reach for.

"Is there life on other planets?"
"Is there a cure for cancer?"
"Can we eliminate disease?"

Some are eternal mysteries. These mysteries lie outside the grasp of human logic. These are the mysteries that scientists don't even try to answer. These are the mysteries that keep both nuclear physicists and 11-year-old girls turning in their beds late at night wondering, just wondering. These are the eternal mysteries that, to the human mind, seem like foolishness, but higher logic will always seem foolish to a lower logic. These are the mysteries that I'm interested in.

God is real and present. He knows your past, present and future. He can watch your birth, see your marriage, observe you playing with your grandchildren, all in the same moment.

HIGHER LOGIC WILL ALWAYS SEEM FOOLISH TO A LOWER LOGIC.

Even before you were formed in your mother's womb, God had a plan for you. He handpicked gifts and created attributes to help you fulfill that plan. He can send a dream to warn you or encourage you. He can send a dream to instruct you and enlighten you as to what is coming next, or about the darkness that wants to prevail over you.

God can also use you to touch others. He can whisper one word in your ear to tell the homeless man in front of you, and the one word will cause him to collapse in a heap and never touch alcohol again.

This same God who sees and knows everything is also interested in even the smallest details of your life. Small details over time can become very large, and large issues keep you from the purpose for which you were created. God doesn't want that.

God speaks to us in a multitude of ways. Sometimes it's the still, quiet voice. Sometimes it's a song on the radio. Sometimes it's the random memory of an old friend. Sometimes it's a riddle. A riddle! Why a riddle?

SMALL DETAILS OVER TIME CAN BECOME VERY LARGE, AND LARGE ISSUES KEEP YOU FROM THE PURPOSE FOR WHICH YOU WERE CREATED. GOD DOESN'T WANT THAT.

This is where understanding dreams and mysteries begin. We realize that God chooses to speak to us through mysteries.

The meanings of dreams are a mystery.

They are God's game of hide and seek. Within His "hiding" and our "seeking" is a relationship that we can develop between each other, creation with Creator.

God says He will not share His glory with another, but it does seem He's made one small exception when it comes to His mysteries:

"It is the glory of God to conceal a matter, But the glory of kings is to search out a matter." Proverbs 25:2

When God conceals matters from us, He's not doing it to withhold something from us. He is issuing an invitation to pursue Him. Dreams are no exception. When we're asleep, God has the opportunity to communicate with us outside of our logical understanding of time and space. He has wisdom to impart to us, but he has to bypass our lower logic to communicate His higher logic. When we dream, God has a captive audience.

WHEN WE DREAM, GOD HAS A CAPTIVE AUDIENCE.

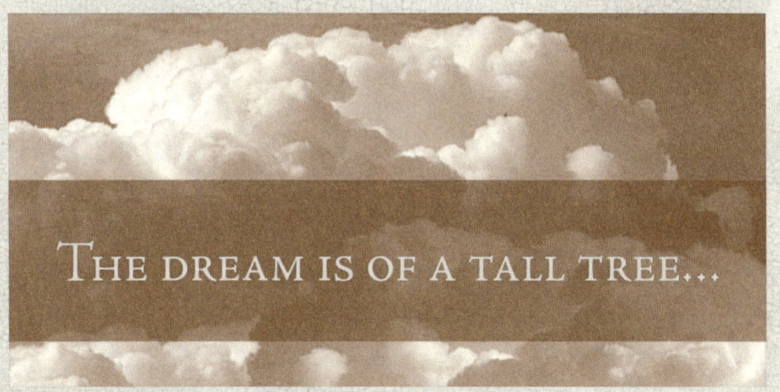

The tree was lush and full and the dreamer was doing aerial aerobics in its branches. It was effortless. Across from the dreamer was the same exact tree, but in it was a coworker, who was copying every move the dreamer made.
The dreamer was quite uncomfortable, feeling the coworker was watching every move in order to copy it and try to do it better. Then the dreamer noticed there was a red cover or blanket in her tree. She felt protected.

This dream is about the dreamer and what she is, or soon will be, going through at work. Trees in dreams often represent leaders. In this dream, she is in a position of trust and favor with a leader at work. She is learning and thriving in this position. At the same time, there is a coworker who is jealous of the dreamer's position and favor. The coworker is trying, or soon will be trying, to take her favor by doing what the dreamer does, only better.

The second thing that is really important is the red blanket. The red blanket tells us that God has given her a blessing and a covering.

The dreamer is being directed to pray for her coworker. God not only loves the dreamer, He also loves the coworker. Whether the coworker is a Christ-follower or not, God loves her. God loved each of us so much that, while we were yet sinners, Christ died for us. The dreamer is to pray that the coworker walks into her own calling and destiny, pray that she recognizes the hand of God on the dreamer's life and doesn't do something that God would have to judge her for later.

When God gives you a dream, He does so because He desires a response from you. Because God created you, He knows the thoughts and intents of your heart. He recognizes when you need His help. However, not all dreams are from God.

There are different types of dreams. There are God dreams, and then there are soul dreams—dreams that you cause based upon your own desires. Have you ever had a dream about winning the lottery? Does this mean you are going to win the lottery? Probably not.

There are also dreams that come from the enemy. The enemy consists of the dark forces that are opposed to what God wants to do through you. These dark forces are committed to stopping God's plans and blocking your destiny. This is where nightmares come from. Why does this happen?

God doesn't give you soul dreams or dark dreams. He doesn't prevent them, either, and He has a good reason for that. Soul dreams reveal truths about you that, if you recognize these truths, you can then change and turn away from.

Dark dreams are a little different. They reveal the plans

of the enemy to stop God's call on your life. Once you see and understand what the enemy has planned, you can then pray and avert or negate those plans.

Dreams are a mystery. You may not always understand the complete meaning of your dreams, but you can always respond. How do you respond? The best way to respond is with prayer. ■

The meanings of dreams are a mystery. They are filled with anticipation and suspense. In one way, they are God's way of playing hide and seek. Think back to when you were a child. What were the feelings you experienced playing hide and seek? When you were the one hiding, you had the suspense and anticipation of being found. When you were the one looking, you felt the thrill of the search. Each time you looked and came up empty, the anticipation and desire for discovery grew.

This is a perfect example of the life God wants with His creation. God has invited you to the ultimate game of hide and seek. It's time to stop counting, open your eyes, and go find Him.

Growing up, I wasn't sure what to believe. I would have dreams about something, and then several days later that very thing would happen. The events that happened weren't anything I could have known or had any control over. It seemed common to me.

Since I read about this happening throughout the Bible, I just assumed God was doing to me what He had done to others before me. But as I would talk to people about dreams, I discovered that not everyone experienced or thought about dreams the same way. I didn't understand why.

That started me on a lifelong journey to understand the meaning of dreams and why God gives them. I felt certain then, and I know for certain now, that I'm not the only one God is speaking to through dreams.

God is speaking to you, always. You have unopened messages from the Creator of everything that has or ever will exist. These messages are tailor-made just for you. These messages are custom-designed for you. But you have to want God to speak, and you have to start searching out the way He speaks. You have to have faith, you have to believe that God does speak to you this way, and then you have to seek out the hidden messages.

DREAMS ARE GOD'S NIGHT PARABLES. THEY WON'T MAKE SENSE IF TAKEN LITERALLY. THAT'S WHY THEY'RE OFTEN IGNORED.

How does God hide from you in dreams? He uses symbols. We can see this in the way Jesus taught us. Jesus taught through parables told in word pictures. Dreams are, after all, God's night parables. The problem is we try to understand a dream by taking the details inside the dream literally, and in doing so often dismiss our dreams as complete nonsense.

Have you ever had a dream about flying? It was probably so real that when you woke up you felt a sense of disappointment when you realized you couldn't fly in real life. In the dream, the experience was probably just amazing. What does that mean?

Flying in dreams is God revealing to you a gift you have to move or experience things of the Spirit. It doesn't mean that you necessarily are having these experiences already. It just means that God has prepared you, and is preparing you, for these things.

FLYING IN A DREAM INDICATES A GIFT TO RISE ABOVE THINGS OF THE EARTH, AND ALSO THE ABILITY TO HAVE SPIRITUAL EXPERIENCES.

What would be the difference between just floating like a balloon, or soaring like an eagle? That would indicate an issue of maturity and the level of training you've received.

What about dreams involving your teeth falling out, or missing, broken, or loose teeth? What could those dreams mean? It's probably not what you think. You're not being chided for not flossing. God may care about hygiene, but that's not what He is getting at in those dreams. In a dream, teeth don't necessarily mean you need to go to the dentist. Teeth represent our ability to "chew" on information, to understand or grasp something. Sometimes you'll go through a period of your life when it's very difficult to chew or process information. I've seen this type of dream repeatedly with college students, particularly pre-med or nursing students.

TEETH FALLING OUT IN DREAMS SPEAKS TO OUR ABILITY TO GRASP AND "CHEW" ON INFORMATION.]

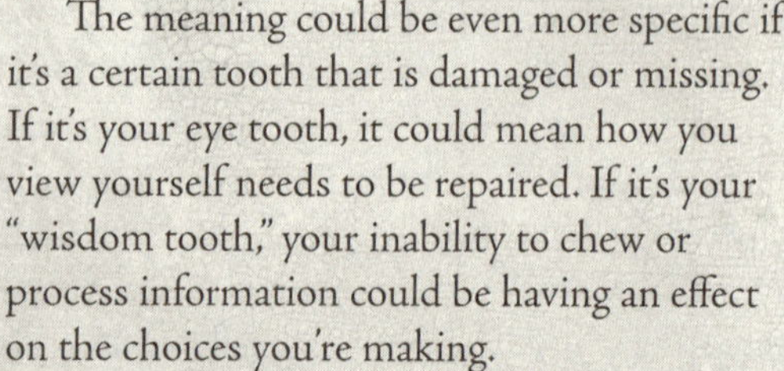

The meaning could be even more specific if it's a certain tooth that is damaged or missing. If it's your eye tooth, it could mean how you view yourself needs to be repaired. If it's your "wisdom tooth," your inability to chew or process information could be having an effect on the choices you're making.

Also on that list of the top 20 dreams are snakes. You would be amazed at how many people have dreams about snakes. What do you think snakes mean in a dream?

THE DREAMER WAS IN HER GREEN-HOUSE AND PULLED OUT A BOX. THE BOX HAD A PLANT AND TOOLS IN IT.

When she lifted the plant out, the box contained four or five snakes of different sizes. The first one jumped out at her, but she was able to avoid it. A couple more left the box, but then she was startled that one had turned into an alligator. The gator stopped right in front of her and stared at her straight in the eye, and the dream ended. What do the snakes mean?

The first thing you want to do when you are interpreting a dream is to walk through the dream story with the person who had the dream. Interpreting a dream starts with how you listen to the dreamer. I don't just listen to the story—I enter the story.

Let's review this dream. There is a greenhouse. There is a plant in a box and tools in a box. There is a snake that jumps out at the person. There are other snakes, and then there is the snake that becomes the alligator.

In a dream, snakes represent lies or "tales" about you. A snake in a dream means a T-A-L-E, not T-A-I-L. The snake signifies a fabrication that someone is making about you. The evil one wants you to start believing it, or have a fear that someone is going to start thinking less of you.

In this dream, the first snake came right at the dreamer's face, but she was able to avoid it. That means the first lie or fabrication is not going to have any results on the dreamer. The venom will not hurt her, the snake's strike will not hit her. It doesn't say what the other snakes are doing, but they are there to avoid.

But the last snake turned into an alligator, and the alligator was sitting there looking straight at the dreamer, right into her eyes. That means the alligator was waiting to see what she was going to do. Alligators are a little more vicious than snakes.

Alligators are meant to take you down. Snakes are meant to hurt you, but alligators are meant to take you down. An alligator's mouth is much bigger than a snake's. The alligator is much more serious.

Our first response is always going to be prayer, but there is one more thing that we may have overlooked at the beginning of this dream. That is, in the box there were tools. God is letting the dreamer know that, no matter what happens, He has given us tools. We have the tools to overcome anything the enemy throws our way. ■

For much of my life, I was the guy who, when people had a dream, they came to me for an interpretation. For years I had no problem being that guy, but one day that all changed. I was with a group of leaders. An Anglican vicar mentioned he had a dream and wondered if anyone at the table could interpret it. Everybody pointed to me, saying without a single word, "That's him. He does that."

The vicar told me his dream, and I interpreted it. The interpretation seemed to resonate with him. Tears came to his eyes. He responded the way lots of people respond, by saying, "How did you do that?"

I told him, as I always did, "It was God."

"I know that," the vicar said, "but how did you do it?"

I said again the standard response I had always given, "It was God."

"I know that, but how did you do it?"

His persistence caused me to realize that there was more to his question than just wanting to know the source of the interpretation. He wanted to know the mechanics of how I arrived at the interpretation.

"I have no idea," I told him, as the glare from his question broke over me. "I honestly have no idea how I do what I do. It's just something God has done with me since my childhood."

"That's too bad," he said, looking at me with clear, piercing eyes, "because when you die, your gift will die with you." Wow! On that same day, I went to the Lord in prayer and asked if I could make a deal with Him. If He would show me the way, the process of interpreting dreams in a way that I could share it with others, then I would devote myself to training others to understand their dreams.

The process is so important. I simply didn't understand it. I would hear the dream, and the meaning would just unfold in my mind. That's great if someone just wants a dream interpreted, but it's not very helpful if they want to learn how to interpret their own dreams.

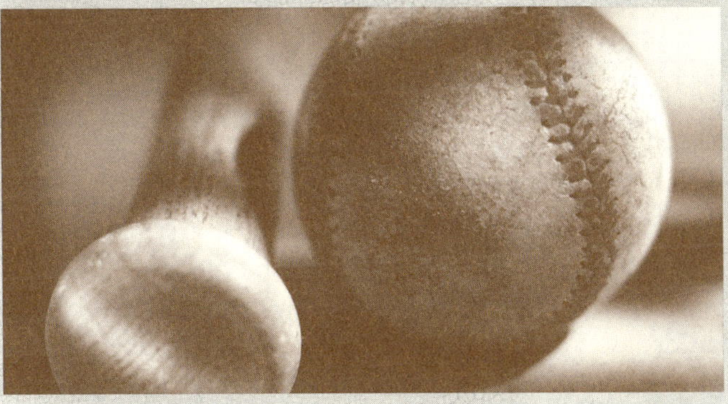

Here's another way to describe it. The best players often make the worst coaches. Let me explain using the sport of baseball.

A hitting coach has the responsibility to teach the process of hitting, the mechanics. They have to be able to break down the experience of hitting. They have to explain the mechanics in bite-sized pieces. That way, when one of their players isn't hitting, the coach can give specific adjustments. The coach knows these adjustments, these tricks and shortcuts, because he had to use them himself.

A star player, on the other hand, is often a natural. The natural can reduce 10 steps in the hitting process to just two: see ball, hit ball. It's those guys who don't really know what they're doing, despite doing it well, who don't make great coaches.

I was a "see ball, hit ball" kind of guy in the area of dream interpretation. To teach others, I had to learn the steps that I was skipping. I had to learn the process.

There is a process to understanding dreams. That process requires an understanding of the metaphorical language God uses in Scripture.

Once you gain that head knowledge of the process, you have to then make sure you don't choke out the spirit knowledge. Head knowledge is what you've learned, spirit knowledge is what the Spirit of God is telling you about the dream.

Think of it like this. Knowledge of Biblical symbolism is like identifying the edges in a jigsaw puzzle. It helps get you started, it helps set the parameters of the meaning of the dream. The Holy Spirit fills in the rest. Dreams turn pictures into words. We can't do that without the help of the Holy Spirit.

Earthly methods, such as Freudian or Jungian dream interpretation, are not the answer for the Christian. It's a

key, but to a different door. We have the Holy Spirit as our teacher and guide.

The Bible states that skill can be given to us.

While I was speaking in prayer, the man Gabriel, whom I had seen in the vision at the beginning, being caused to fly swiftly, reached me about the time of the evening offering. And he informed me, and talked with me, and said, "O Daniel, I have now come forth to give you skill to understand." Daniel 9:21-22

Where do you start? Start by looking at every dream and vision in the Bible. Look for patterns of symbolism to develop. When you read the Psalms and Proverbs, pay close attention to poetic devices like metaphors and similes. They are full of them. In the Psalms, there is hardly a verse where David does not use them. What does the Bible say things are "like"? What word pictures have been placed in the stories and principles?

STEPS TO UNDERSTANDING YOUR DREAMS

Read every dream in Scripture and look for patterns.

Read Proverbs and Psalms and take note of poetic devices and imagery.

Study the parables of Jesus, particularly the ones He explained.

God doesn't include this type of language to impress you or to win critical acclaim. The writers of Scripture, divinely inspired, were not being "paid by the word." They wrote words that are specific clues to the symbolic language of God. God used common words. He didn't search for words that were common to us. He made these items common in order to use the words. His strong desire is to communicate with His beloved creation—you!

Riddles and mysteries are not just found in the Old Testament. Look at the Gospels. See how many times Jesus is asked a question by His disciples and answers with a parable. Time and again Jesus started by saying, "The kingdom of heaven is like..."

In the parable of the seed and the sower, what did the seed represent? It represented the Word of God. Why did the thorns and thistles represent the cares of this world? Because weeds choke out seeds.

This is the invitation God is making to you.

20 Categories of Dreams

Healing Dreams	Flushing Dreams
Calling Dreams	Warning Dreams
False Dreams	Body Dreams
Chemical Dreams	Self-Condition Dreams
Courage Dreams	Correction Dreams
Direction Dreams	Intercession Dreams
Dark Dreams	Prophecy & Revelation Dreams
Spiritual Warfare Dreams	Fear Dreams
Invention Dreams	Word of Knowledge Dreams
Deliverance Dreams	Soul Dreams

God created a world for us in which the most precious elements have to be discovered. Gold is dug out of mountains. Pearls are hidden in the bottom of the ocean, clamped tightly inside shells. In the same way, the "hidden mysteries" of God must be searched out.

It is not satisfying to play hide-and-seek when the person who is supposed to be hiding is standing right behind you, or when the person who is supposed to be seeking never leaves home base. Where is the fun in that? But there is great joy when we seek for something and then find it.

When is the last time God gave you a dream? A bigger question might be, have you been asking God a question?

If you have, then maybe you received your answer last night in a dream and didn't even know it!

How important are dreams, visions and prophecies to God? You may be surprised to know that fully one-third of the Bible is devoted to them!

One-third of the Bible deals with dreams, visions and prophecies. Strange, because we spend one-third of our lives asleep, and God devoted one-third of the Bible to this subject.

As you read today, you've already spent one-third of your life asleep. By the time you are sixty, you will have slept for twenty years. God is the God who never sleeps or slumbers. Is it possible that God may have had something to say in that time?

Every night when you sleep, you dream. You may not remember your dreams when you wake up, but that doesn't mean you didn't dream. It just means you don't remember them. Even the dreams you do remember, if you don't write them down, will fade over time. Dreams are like a novel written with disappearing ink.

Dreams are clearest and most detailed when you first wake up. From that point forward, details of the dream begin to fade. Even the raw emotion you feel right after waking up loses intensity each time you try to recall the dream. It is important to write your dreams down.

Do you want God to speak to you more in dreams? Start writing them down. Writing down your dream does three things:

1. Writing out your dream creates a physical record that you can revisit later.

2. The mere act of writing the details and the storyline of the dream will cause you to use specific words that can become vital to the dream's interpretation later.
3. Writing your dreams shows God that you value what He's giving you. When you value something God has given you, He's justified to give you more. This is one of the mysterious spiritual laws that God has built into the fabric of creation. Spiritual laws, like natural laws, work whether you believe in them or not. "Who is faithful in a very little thing is faithful also in much…if you have not been faithful…who will entrust to you the true riches?" (Luke 16:10-11 Amplified Bible). Start valuing even the seemingly insignificant dreams you have at night and watch what happens. You'll start having vivid, powerful experiences with God in your dreams. I've seen it happen time after time. It starts by valuing this mysterious but powerful gift of God.

DREAMS ARE LIKE A NOVEL WRITTEN WITH DISAPPEARING INK.

God is pouring out His Spirit. He is meeting you and me in a multitude of ways. Dreams are a way of inviting you into a relationship with Him. He's knocking. It's a gentle knock. The world is full of distractions. We have scheduled every waking moment of our lives with something to do, somewhere to go. We've even filled in the pauses and breaks in our lives with handheld technology.

You were not created to be satisfied with this kind of life. The very Spirit of God has breathed into you a memory of an eternal relationship with Him. This memory may be faint, but it's not forgotten. That's why you keep running and never arrive. That's why you eat and never are filled.

Here's what God does. He takes what you give Him. Sometimes He waits until you're asleep, when the busy world cannot distract you. Your logical mind filled with tasks is at rest, and that's when He gives you a dream, but it's not just a dream. The night parable is an invitation to know more about Him by revealing something about you. It is a message from eternity told in a mysterious yet familiar language. Sometimes this message will stay with you your entire life. Sometimes it has been forgotten by lunchtime. Sometimes it is sealed for another time.

One of the most common questions people ask is, "Is God talking to me?"

Here is the simple answer: He is. All the time.

God is knocking with a soft, gentle knock and speaking in a soft, gentle whisper. There is no shortcut to stopping to hear. There is no volume knob that turns God up. You have to turn your own volume up or down.

The dreams and mysteries of God were created for you to discover. We're on this journey together. You won't be disappointed. You were designed with a curiosity that yearns to reach out to your Creator. This is all part of the mystical relationship between Creator and creation.

Reflections and Meditations

Have you ever had a significant dream, one that you never forgot? Can you prayerfully search for an interpretation to it now?

What can you do this week to help you begin to dream?

What can you do to remember your dreams?

What can you do to interpret your dreams?

Use the back of this page to jot down a commitment that you feel in your heart you want to make regarding hearing from God.

CHAPTER 3

THE MYSTERY OF PROPHETS AND PSYCHICS

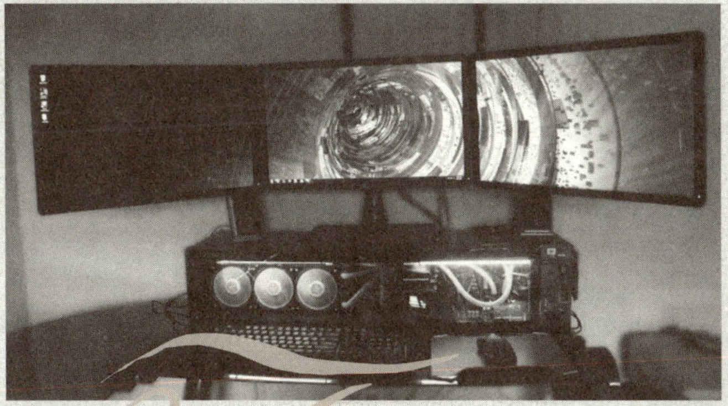

"Futurists" are consultants, social scientists or authors who predict global trends in society. It sounds like a pretty interesting career.

Walk into a living room packed with sports fans on any given weekend, and you'll meet a whole roomful of futurists. Gathering in arenas or homes, sports enthusiasts make prediction after prediction as to what will happen next. Television networks pay announcers to forecast a game's outcome weeks in advance. As they announce the games, they predict what will occur in the very next minute.

The vast majority of sports predictions don't come true. They are often completely off. Yet humans are hardwired to want to know the future, so amateur fans will continue to predict, and networks will continue paying professionals to guess.

What if, through some divine revelation, your predictions did come true and you really did know the future? What does "revelation" even mean? One definition is making secrets known in a dramatic way. Another is gaining knowledge from a source that is beyond our five physical senses. A short one would be spiritual insight.

History is filled with stories of kings who depended on revelation before ships would sail or armies would go to war. Critical decisions involving masses of people were put on hold until revelation came. What about today? Politicians and power brokers are willing to pay whatever it takes to get on top. Once there, they may pay even more to stay.

Necessity may fuel innovation and may be the "mother of invention," but it is revelation that brings such things to life. Revelation can be more valuable than gold, but what determines who gets revelation? Do we all have equal access to it, or is there a special ability, a gift that a few have been given to hear secrets revealed? If so, how do we know who really has this gift? How do we know who just claims to own it?

Revelation is a mystery. We cannot understand the mystery of revelation without looking at the people who receive it, or at least say they do. This is the mystery of prophets and psychics.

I have discovered there are two basic ways of uncovering mysteries. Some mysteries you begin searching out because of a natural curiosity. Other mysteries you stumble into through a variety of ways. Sometimes in the process of solving one problem, a completely different problem arises, and you need an answer to the new one first.

A mystery or problem will sometimes arrive because God

put it there for someone to find, even if they weren't looking for it. It wasn't on their radar, and that was part of the problem. It wasn't on their radar because they didn't know what they didn't know, but God did. This is how it was when I stumbled into this mystery of prophets and psychics.

This kind of mystery, once revealed, is a paradigm shift. A "paradigm" is a pattern or model of something that can potentially shape your worldview.

Jesus was great at shifting people's paradigms. He was probably the greatest paradigm-shifter who ever lived. He made no apologies for it, either. He ate with tax collectors. He asked a Samaritan woman divorced five times to fetch Him water at a well. He allowed a former prostitute to wash His feet with her own hair. Each time this happened, those around Jesus were offended. For those who chose to continue following Him, they witnessed this time and again. It has not changed for those who follow Him now.

Many years ago, on a sunny Southern California afternoon, I had just such a paradigm shift. I found myself with some free time during my visit there, so someone suggested I try rollerblading. They knew the perfect place, Venice Beach. Soon I found myself zipping down Venice Beach Boardwalk on rollerblades. It was exhilarating.

About 15 minutes into my fun, I noticed a signboard that read, "Welcome to the Venice Beach Psychic and New Age Fair." My first thought was "Yikes! I need to stay away from that," but the next thing I perceived was God impressing upon me to turn down that side street and enter the fair. I didn't know that I was about to experience a paradigm shift.

As I was turning around to go back, I figured I knew

what was going on. I thought, "Okay, Lord, You're going to have me skate down this street and really mess up all the psychics trying to do readings, right?" After all, what other reason could God have for me going here?

I went skating through this sidewalk Psychic Fair and heard again, in my spirit, "This one is a fake."

"Of course this one is a fake," was my immediate thought. "They're all fakes!"

Then I passed a booth and heard God impress words deep inside me. "This one has a true gift from Me."

"A true gift? How?" I was stunned. I stood still on my skates, looked at the people in the booth and thought, "WHAT? This cannot be from God!"

Again the Lord clearly spoke to my heart, "This one has a true gift. I gave it to him."

A psychic with a true gift from God? That was a major paradigm shift. I turned in my skates and headed back home, completely deflated. That was the day a mystery I thought I had figured out became a mystery again.

That day on the boardwalk in California ended up changing my life, and that is no exaggeration. I thought I knew all about the gift of prophecy and revelation. I naturally thought that God only gave that gift to someone who followed Him. It made no sense to me that God would give a psychic a gift of revelation.

I was mystified, but also deeply offended. Just as Jesus broke religious molds with His followers when He talked to the prostitute or tax collector, that's what God was after. He wanted to offend my mind to expose my heart. Paradigm shifts often include a violent end to an old point of view.

THE GIFT OF REVELATION IS NOT IN THE MESSAGES THE PERSON IS RECEIVING. THE GIFT IS ONLY THE ABILITY TO RECEIVE THOSE MESSAGES.

For days, I struggled with doubts about the experience and questions about what it could mean. Do prophets and psychics share the same gift from God? After days of prayer, intensely seeking for the answer to this mystery, I finally realized what God was showing me on the boardwalk that day: The gift of revelation is not in the messages the person is receiving. The gift is only the ability to receive those messages.

In other words, the gift is not the signal we receive. It is simply the ability to receive the signal. Understanding this principle becomes a key to understanding what the gift of revelation is later on.

Some psychics have a true prophetic or revelatory gift that originally came from God. The Bible says that the gifts of God are irrevocable. That means that God doesn't remove our gift from us. It's like a government-issued birth certificate.

You get it at the beginning of your life, and it stays with you for the rest of your life.

Does that mean that psychics with true gifts from God are hearing from God when they give their clients readings? Absolutely not! This is important to understand. Psychics are not hearing from God when they are "reading" people. Remember, the gift isn't the signal. The gift is just like "hardware" that allows a person to capture the signal. It's the hardware that is the gift, not the revelation.

THE GIFT ISN'T THE SIGNAL. THE GIFT IS JUST LIKE "HARDWARE" THAT ALLOWS A PERSON TO CAPTURE THE SIGNAL.

By now, you are probably wondering if psychics can have a true revelatory gift from God. The answer is yes, but that does not mean they hear from God. No way! A singer may have a gift of music, but that doesn't mean he or she is singing for God. A person may have a true gift from God, but that doesn't mean he or she hears from God, much less speaks for God.

The gift of revelation is the ability to receive revelation. It can be compared to a satellite dish. The dish represents the gift. The satellite represents God. A satellite dish needs a satellite to communicate with, or else it cannot function the way it was designed to function. A person who knows and serves God is like a satellite dish that is turned and pointed directly to a specific satellite the "God" satellite, we could simply say. This is a picture of how revelation works. When the satellite dish is pointed, signals can beam into that dish. Prophets are attuned to God. Because they serve and follow God, God sends His signal to them in the form of revelation. Psychics, who don't know or serve God, do not receive a signal from God. God may have sent it at one time, but at some point in the psychic's life, the messages from God stopped coming.

One of the great attributes of our God is His incredible mercy. He's not just merciful, He is mercy itself. If God had DNA, mercy would be woven all the way through it. The Bible says God's mercy endures forever.

The Bible also tells us that God is not mocked. When a person lives a life in rebellion to their Creator, there comes a point when God is no longer justified in acting on that person's behalf. God does not stop loving the person. God simply will not extend His mercy to the point where He is no longer just.

One reason God would stop sending a signal to people who were gifted to receive it is because they pulled away from the Giver of the gift. But, once the signal is stopped, God doesn't take the hardware away just because the person chose not to follow Him. That lingering gift or satellite dish will then

PRAISE THE LORD! OH, GIVE THANKS TO THE LORD, FOR HE IS GOOD! FOR HIS MERCY ENDURES FOREVER.

PSALM 106:1

look for an outlet. What used to be full in that person's life becomes empty and leaves a vacuum. A vacuum wants to be filled with something—anything.

Lest we judge these people too harshly, this is a void that can occur with any gift. To the artist it is, "Give me creative vision or else!" To the athlete it is, "Let me compete or else!" To the evangelist it is, "Show me people to share the Gospel with or else!" For a person with a revelatory gift, the pressure is, "Give me revelation or else!" This mysterious gift will then search out other messages. Like a radio that scours the airwaves for some signal that it can pick up, the psychic looks for messages coming from a source other than God.

The mystery of prophets and psychics is that it is the same gift, different sources. God gives gifts, but just as the singer chooses the song to sing, it is up to the person how the gift is used.

In the example of the satellite dish, just imagine what happens if one satellite isn't sending a signal anymore. The psychic looking for another signal eventually finds one.

THE MYSTERY OF PROPHETS AND PSYCHICS IS THAT IT IS THE SAME GIFT, DIFFERENT SOURCES.

There are only two forces—God and not God. That means the signal the psychic finds is from dark forces. Dark forces are always looking for a way to capture someone's gift.

There are psychics in the world today that need to know why they are the way they are. They may have felt early on that they were strange or didn't fit in. They didn't know how to use the gift they were given and didn't have anyone who could teach them. Are they really so different than anyone else misusing a gift from God for their own selfish reasons? Are they any less deserving of our prayers?

Does God love them any less?

The drive to receive direction through some sort of supernatural revelation is a fundamental human need. It is as strong today as it was in the days of the Bible. God is aware of this drive and the danger that it can lead to. That's why so much of the Bible is filled with stories about the dangers of idolatry and the consequences of seeking psychics, wizards and mediums.

God doesn't want us searching for other signals. That is why today we can go to the Source, the Holy Spirit. When we accept Christ, God places His Holy Spirit inside us. For some, they don't want the relationship or commitment that the Holy Spirit asks. They just want an answer, any answer.

How are my stocks going to do? Is my husband cheating on me? Will I see my pet in Heaven? What do I need to do to get the big promotion?

These are all questions that drive people to psychics. Do they get answered? Yes and no. Yes, they get answered, or else the psychic wouldn't get paid! But is it the right answer, or does the answer make the person's life any better? No, not at all.

Psychics, mediums, and tarot card readers all depend on dark beings called "familiar spirits" to communicate information to their unsuspecting victims. Yes, victims.

Familiar spirits are demonic beings that share information with each other and then make that information available to a psychic, medium or other kind of "seer." They are not all-powerful or all-knowing. They cannot read minds, but they don't have to. They just gather information from what they see and hear. Because this dark network has been in place longer than we have, knowing the past is no obstacle.

Familiar spirits can state the nickname that someone's great grandmother had for the great grandfather. Imagine how impressed someone might be to have a psychic tell them that detail.

That's the plan. Sharing information that plays on the pain and fears of others is the game. Sharing information that can be used to manipulate, or sharing information that will cause the psychic to gain influence and credibility so customers keep returning, it is all about control and manipulation.

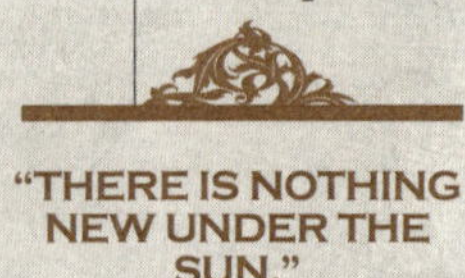

"THERE IS NOTHING NEW UNDER THE SUN."
ECCLESIASTES 1:9

This is what happened in the Old Testament when King Saul grew impatient to get answers and sought out a witch at Endor.

"And when Saul inquired of the Lord, the Lord did not answer him, either by dreams or by Urim or by the prophets" (1 Samuel 28:6). In this story, first we see that kings expected to hear from God either by dreams, or by the stones the priests carried, or by prophets such as Samuel. Saul wasn't getting an answer through the usual means, so he had one of his men find a psychic, and God stripped the kingdom from him as a result.

In the New Testament, Paul and Silas had a woman with a spirit of divination follow them. She kept yelling out that these were servants of the most high God and would show the people the way to salvation. At first glance we might say, "What's so wrong with that? What she was saying was true."

Paul discerned that something wasn't right about the spirit in which she was making this proclamation. This woman wasn't trying to glorify God or lead people to salvation, she was trying to show off that she was the one with discernment about Paul and Silas, so that after they left the people would look to her. Paul put a quick end to it and silenced her.

Familiar spirits get two things out of their relationships with psychics. First, they get an indentured servant in the form of the psychic. Dark spirit beings want, more than anything, to possess a physical being. They love being invited in, and they hate leaving.

Jesus cast out a "legion" of spirits from a demoniac in the country of the Gadarenes. Those spirits pleaded with Him to send them into some nearby swine. To a dark spirit, even possessing an animal is better than nothing.

Make no mistake, it might be the psychic's name on the sign and on the bank account, but the familiar spirit is the boss. A dark spirit is a harsh taskmaster, and it makes the psychic the slave.

Familiar spirits will do and say anything to remain in control of the person they possess. They'll even say something that appears to be righteous. These Bible passages show us how the spirit of divination hides as a wolf in sheep's clothing.

The same thing happens today when psychics work with police departments to find missing people. At face value, this looks like a noble cause, but looks can be deceiving. This is why the Bible says we are to test the spirit. The Spirit of God inside of us will tell us when someone is operating out of a false spirit. We often forget that the Holy Spirit is the Spirit of Truth. We learn to recognize truth by the peace that it leaves inside us.

To receive a reading from a psychic is to ask advice from a dark spirit that ultimately wants your demise. It will throw the psychic into its prison in order to keep the psychic's customers from following God's plan for their lives. Listening to a psychic is ultimately listening to a plan that only leads to destruction.

The second thing the familiar spirit gets through a relationship with a psychic is access to the person the psychic is "reading." It is like a two-for-one sale. The familiar spirit uses the psychic as a bridge to gain access to the psychic's customers.

This can be compared to something like a computer virus. A person goes to a psychic. The psychic asks the person's permission to search his or her "hard drive." Information gets unknowingly downloaded or exchanged. A couple of weeks later, weird things start popping up in the person's life. People who have had their computers infected with a virus understand this. It's the same thing with psychics. We don't want what they have to infect our lives.

Familiar spirits are not anything to joke about. We must not be tricked into thinking psychics and tarot cards or Ouija boards are just a form of entertainment. They are not. When people consult with these things, they are actually engaging in witchcraft. They are playing on the enemy's turf and inviting dark spirits into their lives. They are asking a demon to tell them the future when they should be asking God.

My studies of Scripture have convinced me that a person who is born again cannot be possessed by a demon. However, any of us can be harassed and oppressed by a demon. For example, addictions such as drugs, pornography or alcohol all have demonic oppression issues involved.

Consulting psychics is one way to open the door for

demonic harassment. If you have made the mistake of visiting a psychic or tarot card reader, or played around with a Ouija board or any of these dark things forbidden in scripture, there are steps to take to close the doors that were opened in your life.

Today, the same desperation we saw in King Saul to hear from God is very much alive. There is desperation in people today to hear from God.

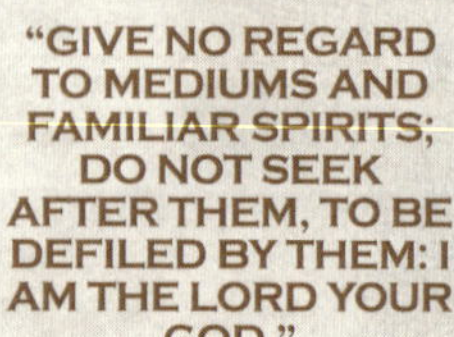

"GIVE NO REGARD TO MEDIUMS AND FAMILIAR SPIRITS; DO NOT SEEK AFTER THEM, TO BE DEFILED BY THEM: I AM THE LORD YOUR GOD."

LEVITICUS 19:31

What about those people, Christians maybe, who grow impatient and get tired of waiting on God for an answer so they consult psychics and the familiar spirits they carry? The fact is, they have asked a dark being to see the future. They have engaged with those who are God-cursed and removed from Heaven. This now gives tacit permission for those dark beings to do whatever they want in that person's life.

One passage of Scripture reads, "My people are destroyed for lack of knowledge" (Hosea 4:6). Some people today go to church, claim Christ as their Lord and Savior, and still think it is okay to visit psychics. That has to stop. This is not entertainment. It gives demonic spirits license to wreak havoc in their lives.

What will happen to them now? What can they do? God's mercy is more than big enough to forgive them, but they have to acknowledge the wrong in their actions. If this is you or somebody you know, here are some simple steps that help close the doors that may have been opened.

First, you have to repent and ask God to forgive you for turning to another source to receive direction.

Second, you need to come out of agreement with everything that was spoken over you during those encounters.

Third, you need to ask God to reveal any open doors that the enemy has gained from that encounter, and then ask God to close those doors.

Fourth, it is important to forgive. Forgive anyone, including the psychic, who you may have judged or still hold something against. Unforgiveness can keep God from acting on your behalf.

It is also important to forgive yourself for visiting the psychic in the first place. Forgiving yourself is very important. Once you ask God for forgiveness, there's no need to carry guilt or condemnation for those decisions. If God has forgotten it, so should you.

CLOSING THE DOOR TO FAMILIAR SPIRITS

1. Ask God to forgive you
2. Come out of agreement from the encounter
3. Ask God to reveal every open door, then ask God to close those doors
4. Forgive anyone, including yourself

When you take these important steps, you start a process of recovery. You'll see your life change, a weight lifted, and find yourself back on the right track.

Revelation and information are not the same. Information might be very interesting and tickle the ears, but information is like yesterday's newspaper. It already happened, and you're just now hearing about it. Revelation has the power to shape and change the future.

Familiar spirits will often try to make information look like revelation. One of the ways they do that is by making their customer think they're telling the future in order to keep that person coming back.

I had an experience in my early twenties that illustrates this point perfectly. I walked into an apartment office looking for an apartment to rent. When I walked in, the apartment manager looked at me. She pushed herself away from her desk, stood and came toward me saying, "Oh my, you have a gift."

At first, I thought they were having some kind of a birthday party and were expecting someone to bring the presents. I said, "No, I don't have a gift. I'm just here looking for an apartment."

"No, you have a gift," she said, "you really have a gift." "No," I said, "I really don't have a gift. I'm just here looking for an apartment."

"No, you have a gift. Here, let me see your watch."

I gave her the cheap watch I was wearing, and she started rubbing it. The more she rubbed it, the more a strange look came over her face. Then she said something incredibly startling to me.

"There is a young woman you have been dating, and you thought something might come of that relationship, but it's broken now. By the way, her first name begins with (let's say) the letter X and her last name begins with the letter Y, and you're going to receive a letter from that girl within the next two or three days."

Then she stopped, handed me back my watch, and said, "Well, that's all I have, here."

I was surprised because I had briefly dated a woman who fit that description. Three days later I really did receive a letter from that woman wanting to get back together with me.

The truth was, the demonic forces had seen something. They made it look like revelation, but it was really only information. The dark spirits had seen the woman writing the letter. They knew it would take about two or three days to get to me. Put the letter and the mail time together, and when it was conveyed to me, it looked like they knew the future. It looked like this apartment manager knew the future, but she didn't. It was yesterday's news that I just hadn't read yet.

I walked out of her office that day and told her, "I don't think this is the apartment complex I'm looking for."

On my way to the car, I tossed the watch into the dumpster. No way did I want any association with that manager.

All she gave me was yesterday's news masquerading as the future. There is a great difference between revelation and information.

God has given each of us unique gifts. Some have been given a gift to receive revelation, to know things almost out of thin air, but the gift of revelation is never about the gift. The gift of revelation is always about the divine Gift Giver. The gift and its revelatory message have to be about the Source.

Without the Source, it is not a gift at all.

In life you will encounter difficult decisions, decisions that seem too big for you, decisions that require you to look beyond what you know at the present time. Sometimes the answer may be hidden. God wants you to know what these answers are, he wants you to know the secrets, but the secrets can only be discovered through a relationship with Him.

While some may have been given the gift of revelation, all of us can hear from God. You can hear from God. Just take time to be quiet and get away from the things that distract you. Press in deeper to Him, and the questions you're asking will be answered. You'll recognize it from the peace you feel inside.

"And let the peace of God rule in your hearts."
Colossians 3:15

Reflections and Meditations

Have you watched television programs that feature psychics or mediums? Have any of those been your favorite shows?

Do you think mediums are real? Have you ever been to one? Have you ever been to a tarot card reader or played with a Oijua board? Did you think there was any danger in doing that?

How did this chapter affect how you think about such things?

How can you learn to exercise the gifts God has given you?

How can you close any doors you may have accidentally opened to dark forces of evil? Will you do that today?

CHAPTER 4

THE MYSTERY OF GOOD AND EVIL

The battle between good and evil, is there really such a thing? What is evil anyway? How could God allow evil to exist?

A battle exists, yes, but it is much more than that. It's a rivalry. Two foes have been locked since the beginning of recorded time. How did this battle, this rivalry between good and evil start?

When Satan rebelled against God? No. Satan and God aren't rivals. God is too big for him. God isn't fighting with

Satan for control of anything. The rivalry between good and evil started in a garden.

There were two trees in the Garden of Eden. There were actually lots of trees in the Garden. It was a lush, beautiful garden, and it was perfect. If you happened to be a stranger just passing through this garden and asked for directions to the tree, chances are the couple tending the place knew what you were talking about. They could give you specific directions to two trees.

One tree was called the Tree of Life. It had a well-worn pathway all the way up to its branches. On it hung fruit that allowed you to live forever. This would make this tree very important to remember.

In the Garden was another tree, the Tree of the Knowledge of Good and Evil. There was a path to it as well. Its path wasn't as worn, and it didn't lead all the way to the tree's branches. Its path stopped just within eyesight.

Over time, the path to one tree had grown a little wider, while the path to the other tree had grown just a little longer.

From the very beginning of man's existence on earth there has been a struggle, the struggle between good and evil. There was a period of time before the real struggle started. During that time, God walked with Adam in the Garden in the cool of the day. I'm sure there was a bit more to it than just a walk. After all, God didn't need the exercise.

At some point, Eve was created. She probably joined Adam and God for some of these walks. I wonder if the subject of that other tree ever came up? I know I'd have some questions about it.

First, why is it even here if we're not supposed to eat from it, and why would you give us a choice if the result of that choice is death? Wouldn't it be better if that other tree wasn't even in the Garden? Or if it has to be here, why does it have to be so appealing? Why does it have to look so good?
All of these would have been great questions to ask during these walks with God in the cool of the day, but Scripture seems to indicate Adam and Eve never sought further clarification. There was only one rule in paradise. Maybe they just didn't want to complain about that one rule, at least not to God.

God not only loves you, He wants you to love Him. He doesn't want to be loved out of obligation, He wants to be loved out of a freewill decision. He wants you to choose to love Him. That's why there were two trees in the garden. Without the Tree of the Knowledge of Good and Evil, there was only one choice, which is no choice at all.

WHY WERE THERE TWO TREES IN THE GARDEN?

Love has to be a freewill decision
God wanted Adam and Eve to have a choice
Without a choice, we're just robots

God created humanity with a need to be chosen. None of us want a relationship with a friend or spouse that takes place without the ability to choose. We all want to be loved. We want to be chosen for who we are. It is that very reality, that a person has a choice to be with us or not be with us, that makes us feel loved. What satisfies the craving of our hearts for companionship is the fact that people could choose not to like us, or not be attracted to us, or not look forward to spending time with us. If we thought for a moment that our friend or spouse was doing it for any other reason than by choice, it wouldn't feel the same. No one wants a robot for a wife or husband, and God feels the same way.

The relationship between good and evil is itself a mystery.

First, there is God. He sent His Son to redeem the world and pay for the consequences of sin once and for all. Jesus took back the authority that was given to Satan in the Garden and returned it to mankind. Jesus was justified in doing so by accomplishing what Adam and Eve could not. Jesus said no to Satan.

Then there is Satan. After thousands of years in control of the earth, he had to return the authority he received from Adam back to man when Jesus came. The Apostle Paul called Jesus the "Last Adam." Satan had to hand over authority because Jesus lived a sinless life.

That happened 2,000 years ago, but today Satan is still here. He still is allowed to exist, and he still has power. Why?

He knows there are men in his house. They are going to each room in the dreamer's house and killing members of his family, but he can't get out of bed to help. It's like he's stuck to his bed. He tries to scream, but nothing comes out. He can hear the screams from down the hall, but he can't do anything about it. When the dreamer knows they are just about to get to his room,

he suddenly wakes up.

In every dark dream there is one common denominator: fear. Some dark dreams communicate fear through a subtle feeling of uncertainty or trepidation. Some induce panic, indecision and confusion. Others are the classic nightmare where you're being chased, someone you love is being harmed, or you're being forced to do something you're afraid to do in real life.

In this dream, the enemy is attacking the dreamer's faith. The enemy is attacking the very idea that the dreamer has the power to stop the plans of the enemy in his life. He can't move or take action. He can't scream or call out for help.

If the enemy can convince you that you have no power to overcome him, you'll simply stop trying to overcome him. That is the enemy's goal.

Dark dreams are given to you by the enemy for one reason: to stop the plans of God in your life. Fear kills faith. You can't experience fear and faith at the same time. When one turns on, the other turns off.

Dark dreams can target specific areas of your life that the enemy wants to target and neutralize. Dark dreams are sent to scramble your spiritual radar by taking your focus off of what God is doing and on what the enemy is doing. ■

The enemy gives dark dreams to:
Stop the plans of God in your life through fear.
Target specific areas of your life that are a threat to evil.
Cause you to never want to dream again.

And finally, dark dreams are sent to try to scare the dreamer into not wanting to ever dream again. Some dreamers learn to hate dreams. Many people who have experienced recurring nightmares have made a vow to themselves to never dream again, and this is exactly what the enemy wants.

But why does God allow dark dreams? Could there actually be a glimmer of hope in even the most terrifying of nightmares? The answer is "yes!"

A man came over to where she was sitting, then he got up and came right up to her. He looked at her and said, "I really, really cannot stand the sound of your voice." The dreamer didn't think anyone else could hear him, but he was in her face speaking the words. Then she woke up, and it compelled her to start to worship. Her worship flowed freely. It was as if the attempted attack caused her to soar to a new level of worship. ■

When you look at the world today, you could arrive at the conclusion that it is becoming darker and more evil by the day. That would be an understandable conclusion. You could also conclude that Satan has more influence in the world than ever. It would seem logical to believe Satan has more influence than God.

It even seems that Satan has power over our dreams. How can that be? How can a time that God uses to speak and encourage us also be accessible to a being that only wants to steal, kill and deceive everyone?

The reason has to do with the very nature of God and how His Kingdom works.

If God is perfect, and He is, then His justice also has to be perfect. The scales of justice always have to be in balance. When God gives us a dream, and reveals to us something we couldn't see or understand without the dream, He in essence tips the scales in our favor. To balance them, He allows the enemy a measure of access to our dreams.

From our last dream example, you can see that even nightmares can serve God's purposes. They reveal the plans of the enemy. They highlight the gifts God has given you. You may not even be aware of those gifts.

A dream from the enemy that is interpreted uncovers the strategy of the forces of evil. Evil always wants to destroy the plans of God. Evil does this by identifying and then attacking those with spiritual gifts, the very gifts God has given you to advance the Kingdom of God.

DARK DREAMS TIP THE HAND OF SATAN BY REVEALING HIS PLANS.

You were created to be a destroyer of evil. That is what advancing the Kingdom of God is—it means destroying evil. That's why Jesus came. Jesus came to demonstrate how we as humans can destroy the works of evil on earth.

As you might imagine, evil isn't particularly thrilled at this prospect. That's what gives evil the motivation to oppose you. Evil wants to destroy the very thing that was created to destroy it. Its best weapon is lies. Lies about you, lies about God, even lies about evil itself.

JESUS CAME TO DEMONSTRATE HOW WE CAN DESTROY THE WORKS OF EVIL ON EARTH.

Let's dispel the lies with some facts about Satan.

First, his name is not Satan. Satan is a title. Satan is a Hebrew word that means "overseer of Hell," "decayer" or "taker of life."

His name is also not Lucifer. Lucifer is a Babylonian word that means "adversary that comes as light." Satan is a title, not a name. Satan did have a name, but God removed it from existence when Satan and one-third of the heavenly beings rebelled and God kicked them out of Heaven.

Second, contrary to what Satan might have you believe, he does not know your thoughts. He also does not know the future. That would mean he is omniscient. Omniscience is the ability to know everything. How do we know he's not omniscient? Because if Satan was all-knowing, he wouldn't have rebelled against God, because he would have known he would lose.

THE TRUTH ABOUT SATAN

1. Satan is not a name. It is a title. His name is not Lucifer. Satan's name was removed forever when he rebelled.
2. Satan does not know your thoughts. Satan does not know the future. If he did, he never would have rebelled, because he would have known he would lose.
3. Satan is not omnipresent. He can only be in one place at one time.
4. Satan is not omnipotent. He has no authority unless you give it to him.

This is proof that the "nameless one" cannot read your thoughts.

Third, Satan is not omnipresent. He can only be in one place at a time. Like other spiritual beings, he can move at the speed of thought. But Satan can only be at one place at a time. That's why it is highly unlikely that he would possess a human being, because he would be restricted in movement to wherever that person could go.

Fourth, Satan is not to be feared. Satan has no power or authority in your life that you don't give him.

To be a light in a dark world, you will encounter darkness. Here are two simple truths that will help you understand the spiritual realm.

What we focus on we make room for. If we focus on darkness, its presence, its power around us, then we've just created a space for it to operate in our lives.

When you focus on God, you are telling evil that God is in charge, and you provide God the space to do that very thing.

We cannot allow ourselves to be naïve to the strategies of the enemy. Too often, we give the enemy credit for something he has no power and no authority to do. What we focus on we make room for. Never focus on a lower power.

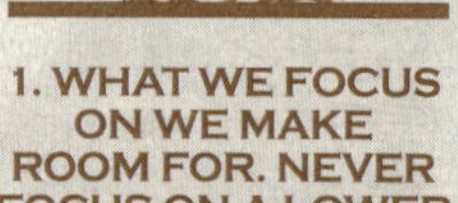

1. WHAT WE FOCUS ON WE MAKE ROOM FOR. NEVER FOCUS ON A LOWER POWER.
2. WHAT WE FEAR WE EMPOWER. FEAR GIVES POWER TO THE PERSON OR OBJECT WE FEAR.

The second truth is this: what we fear we empower. Fear gives power to the person or object we fear. That's why the enemy wants us to be afraid of him. That's why I love when I hear the term "fear of God." When you fear God, you're giving God the power to control your life.

Fear of God, Proverbs tells us, is the beginning of wisdom. It is the release of a type of wisdom that is not from this world. It is a release that comes from the throne of God rather than education or experience. The "fear of God," our awesome reverence toward Him, puts us and God in proper alignment. This pushes the enemy right out of your life.

"You are the light of the world. A city that is set on a hill cannot be hidden. Nor do they light a lamp and put it under a basket, but on a lampstand, and it gives light to all who are in the house. Let your light so shine before men, that they may see your good works and glorify your Father in heaven."
Matthew 5:14-16

Have you ever walked into a room and noticed someone that just seemed brighter than everybody else? You can be that person.

You are the light of the world. Remember that. Light has matter, density, speed, substance. Darkness has none of those things. Darkness is merely the absence of light. You can't release darkness in a bright room and make it less bright. You can release light in a dark room and make it lighter.

You have the ability to release light wherever you go. I'm not talking about a symbolic light. I'm talking about a real, tangible light. A light that when you walk in a room makes you stand out among a crowd just because of the light you carry.

Let me give you an example. I was standing in a grocery store buying shampoo, something very average. I was looking for shampoo among the myriad of shampoos to choose from. In the corner of my eye, I saw a woman walk by. She was walking with a little girl. I saw her walk by again, and then finally walk right up to where I was. I figured she was looking for shampoo, too.

I didn't want to be rude to her, so I moved over and allowed her to see the shampoos. I finally picked up the one I had chose and started to walk off, but she stopped me.

"Excuse me," she said. "Can I ask you a question? Would you pray for me?"

"Sure," I said. "I'd be happy to pray for you, but why did you even ask that?"

"I don't know," she said. "I was walking by, and I saw a light around you. I turned around and walked by again, and I saw it again. Then I turned around and came back, and I see this light. I just had this feeling that if you would pray for me, God would hear your prayers. Would you pray for me and my little girl?"

She then told me what she wanted to pray about. Right there in the grocery store, in the shampoo aisle, we prayed and God touched that woman and her little girl.

Everywhere you go, you can change the atmosphere around you if you have faith to believe that greater is He that lives in you than he that lives in the world. The light God gives you will be noticed by the world.

The enemy, the entire collection of invisible forces of evil that hate God, has a lot to lose. The enemy doesn't want you to know that you have this light. The forces of evil will use all manner of intimidation, lies and temptations to stop you from walking in the power and authority God has given you.

Light will always conquer darkness. Darkness is nothing.

Darkness is not a substance. It has no weight or mass.

Darkness is merely the absence of light.

When you light a candle in a dark room, doesn't the room get lighter? Inside a closed box, there is no light, but what happens when you open it? Does the room you are in get darker? No, the room doesn't get darker! The darkness that was inside this box meets the light, and the box becomes full of light.

The "light of the world" that is in you operates in the same way. You are a light. When you come in contact with darkness, you don't become dark because of that darkness. Darkness becomes enlightened because of you.

When this truth sinks into our hearts, we live our lives differently. We become more focused on what God is doing, and less concerned with what the enemy is doing.

If darkness isn't a substance, what is it?

Darkness, or evil, is not only the absence of light—it's the absence of the source of light. When God kicked one-third of the heavenly beings out of Heaven, He removed those beings from His presence. From that point forward, they began deteriorating. Separation from God is deterioration. Sin is separation from God. The effect of sin, then, is deterioration.

For this very reason, it seems like evil is flourishing. As an individual, a family, a neighborhood, a city, a country gets separated from God, it deteriorates. We lose wisdom, we lose ground, God's hand of protection lifts. He has given us the free will to choose between good and evil, holy and profane, light and dark.

That brings us to a critical truth to understand: God has never made a defensive move. He has never sat around in Heaven watching earth as if on a television. He has never said, "Wow! I didn't see that coming!" He has never felt the need to put a better plan in place to keep something from happening again.

You became a "new creation" when you believed on Jesus Christ. That means you don't have to live your life responding to the moves of the enemy, either. Instead, you can be the force, the agent of change that puts the enemy on the defensive.

Remember that you have the Spirit of God inside you. You've been given gifts that tip the scales. You have the ability to affect others with those gifts without even saying a word because of the light and the Spirit of God you carry.

Here is a critical point to understand. God sent His Son in the "fullness of time." The fullness of time didn't mean the time when the Light of God covered the entire earth. When Jesus came, it was the darkest time the earth had ever experienced.

The fullness of time is right now, right where you are. The darker it gets, the more your light can shine. We can see farther in the darkness than in the daylight, because at night we can see all the way to faraway stars with the naked eye. God chose you to be alive at this very time to spread your light to a world that is filling with darkness.

How do you prepare yourself to be a light to the world? First, know and understand more about the God of Lights. Holiness is not something that comes from what we do or what we don't do. Holiness is attained by being—living, abiding—in the presence of the One who is Holy. There is only One who is holy, and that is God.

Second, know and understand that you are precious to God. He really cares for you.

"The moment you began praying, a command was given.

And now I am here to tell you what it was, for you are very precious to God." Daniel 9:23, New Living Translation

God has planted the seed of His Spirit inside you, and every time you agree with Him about who you are, that seed is fertilized and watered. Harvest will come forth. In the right season and in the right way, it will happen. Whatever you need to accomplish God's purpose, God will do. He will move Heaven and Earth to help you get there.

One thing that helps me is declarative prayer. When I pray declarative prayer over myself, these things happen. Here is what I want to pray over you today. These are things the Scripture says about you:

- You are the light of the world, because the Light of the World dwells in you.
- You will bear God's light to change the world.
- You will become increasingly aware of the Light of God that you carry.
- You will grow in God and grow in His Light.
- God's Kingdom will come, God's will, will be done in you as it is in Heaven.
- No one will meet you and not be changed, because of God's Spirit in you.
- You will become a change agent in this world.
- You will believe the unbelievable; what is not yet you will become.
- You will come to understand who you are in God, and you will see your future more clearly than ever before.
- The gifts you have been given will begin to flourish as You understand God's ways.
- Nothing will prosper that comes against you, because you

will live a repentant life before God.

- You will become what God has called you to become.
- You have been placed here for such a time as this.
- You live where you live because God placed you here.
- You are not here by accident; you are here by divine appointment.

DECLARATIVE PRAYER IS ONE OF THE MOST POWERFUL FORMS OF PRAYER.

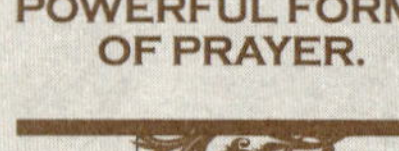

- Your neighbors will prosper because of God in you.
- Where you work will prosper because of God in you.
- Those you touch will prosper because of God in you.
- God's Spirit will flow through you, therefore it is impossible for you to pray for anyone and them not be touched; it makes no difference if they recognize it or not — God will touch them.
- God will sometimes touch others more than at other times; you will not judge your relationship with God based solely on what they feel.
- You relate to God because God's Spirit is in you, not because of what others say, not because of your emotions, not because you feel saved, not because you've ascended to anything — but because of what God has done in you.
- You are procreated, regenerated and born anew.
- God's seed of light has entered you.
- Your spirit is alive and quickened because God's breath is in you.
- You will become quickened to God, fine-tuned to God's Spirit, not doing what God is not doing and doing what God is doing.

- You will become a witness for God because God's light in you proves to others that God exists.
- With God's help, when people see you they will see the Father.
- Soon there will be a clear distinction between those who don't know God and you because you know God.
- People will look at you, and they will know that you are a follower of Jesus and a bearer of His Light.
- For God's glory this will happen, taking the foolish things to confound the wise.
- All because you are growing closer to God.

When you pray declarative prayer in this manner, the power of God flows through you in greater measure, unencumbered and unrestricted. It will increasingly become less encumbered and flow at greater rates, greater speeds, to change people's lives and advance the glorious Kingdom of the Lord Jesus Christ within and through me. It will increase evermore. It will continue to increase and flow at greater rates, like a crescendo, to flow and to help change people's lives.

God has determined the pre-appointed time for your life, the exact place where you would dwell, the exact time that you would be born, the exact geographic location where you can fulfill what He has called you to fulfill. He has placed you where you are in order to touch and change that area where you live. The enemy—the powers of darkness—will be broken because of the power of the Living God upon you.

God understands that there are times when you feel you can't find Him. There are times when you feel that you're groping for Him aimlessly, perhaps. He is not far from you! He does this, because it draws you closer to Him. In that random search, asking "Where is God?" in that moment, you will find Him. He has orchestrated creation and you, His creature, so that you would search for Him. He wants you to seek for Him that, in hope, you might find Him, and He is there.

"FOR IN HIM WE LIVE AND MOVE AND HAVE OUR BEING, AS ALSO SOME OF YOUR OWN POETS HAVE SAID, 'FOR WE ARE ALSO HIS OFFSPRING.'"
ACTS 17:28

That's part of this whole mystery of good and evil on earth, that is, the battle between two kingdoms. That battle takes place in both the physical and spiritual realms simultaneously. There are things we see and things we don't.

Generally, we spend way too much time focused on what we see and not enough time on the spiritual world that we can't see—which is really the "superior world." We also concede far too much power to the enemy. We don't even know it. We don't see ourselves as God sees us. Because of this, we limit God's power to work through us.

When I go out on the streets or to pagan places to reach people for Christ, I keep reminding myself of this incredible, invisible light we carry. Often, people from the New Age community will come up to me and say, "What amazing aura you have." Could they be describing this light we're talking about? Are they really just seeing the light of God? This is the light that Jesus said all Christians will have.

Should Christians have auras, or could it be that an aura is just a counterfeit word for the light of God that God has created in you and me? It is a light that grows in us and in anyone who draws close to God. They see it from their darkness, the light of the world shining through.

Could it be that we allow ourselves to be afraid of something that the world has assigned a counterfeit name to that is really a gift from God?

"Let your light so shine before men, that they may see your good works and glorify your Father in heaven."
Matthew 5:16

Reflections and Meditations

Have you watched television programs that feature psychics or How does this unfolded mystery help you to understand how to identify evil?

Has evil tried to take over your life?

Have you ever had a "dark dream" from the enemy? Now that you have identified it, what purpose can it serve you in your relationship with God?

How can you let your light shine to the world around you?

What "declarative prayer" will you start praying over yourself today?

CLASS IS IN SESSION!

with John Paul Jackson's Online Classroom

Take one or all four university-caliber courses written by John Paul Jackson. It's never been easier to take a quantum leap forward in your spiritual walk. Each of these 23-hour courses can be streamed right from your computer, tablet or smartphone. Learn in-depth:

The Art of Hearing God
Understanding Dreams and Visions
Prayer and Spiritual Warfare
Living the Spiritual Life

Begin your journey to understand all God has for you by going to StreamsMinistries.com. Click on "Online Classroom."

Get all these great resources from Streams Ministries!

About the Author

John Paul Jackson is recognized as a minister who reveals God, awakens dreams, and leads people to Christ and closer to God. For over 30 groundbreaking years, he has been known as an authority on biblical dream interpretation.

He renews passion in people of various faiths and age groups with his sincere explanations of the unexplainable mysteries of life, and enables people to relate to God and others in fresh and meaningful ways.

As an inspirational author, international speaker, insightful teacher of true spirituality, television guest, and host of his own television program, *Dreams and Mysteries*, John Paul has enlightened thousands of people across the world. He finds satisfaction in his role as a youth mentor, advisor to church and national leaders, and the promotion of the spiritual arts.

@JohnPaulJackson
Facebook.com/JPJFanPage
StreamsMinistries.com